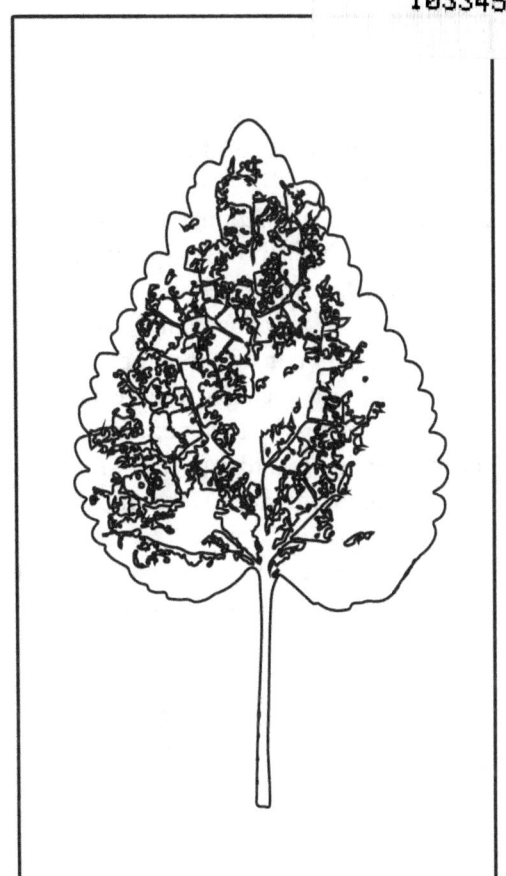

Copyright © 2022 Michèle Saint-Michel
All rights reserved.
10 9 8 7 6 5 4 3 2 1

Published by Bad Saturn. BAD SATURN and associated logos are trademarks and/ or registered trademarks.

All rights reserved under International and Pan-American Copyright Conventions. No part of this publication may be reproduced, transmitted, downloaded, decompiled, reverse engineered, or stored in or introduced into any information storage and retrieval system, in any form or by any means, whether electronic or mechanical, now known or hereafter invented, without the express written permission of the publisher. For information regarding permissions, email Bad Saturn, Attention: Permissions Department.

The publisher does not have any control over and does not assume any responsibility for author or third-party websites or their content.

LIBRARY OF CONGRESS
CATALOGING-IN-PUBLICATION DATA

Saint-Michel, Michèle.
Journeywork of the Stars: A Dotted Journal
/ by Michèle Saint-Michel.
— 1st ed.
p.
Crn.
ISBN: 978-0-9999020-6-6

Summary:
A dotted journal with freedom to dream. Based on the work of intermedia artist and poet Michèle Saint-Michel, this dotted journal creates space for bullet journaling, notes, thought bubbles, and boxes. A gift for yourself or anyone who sees extraordinary freedom in the stars.

Space and Time! now I see it is true,
what I guess'd at,
What I guess'd when I loaf'd on the grass,
What I guess'd while I lay alone in my bed,
And again
as I walk'd the beach

under the paling stars of morning.

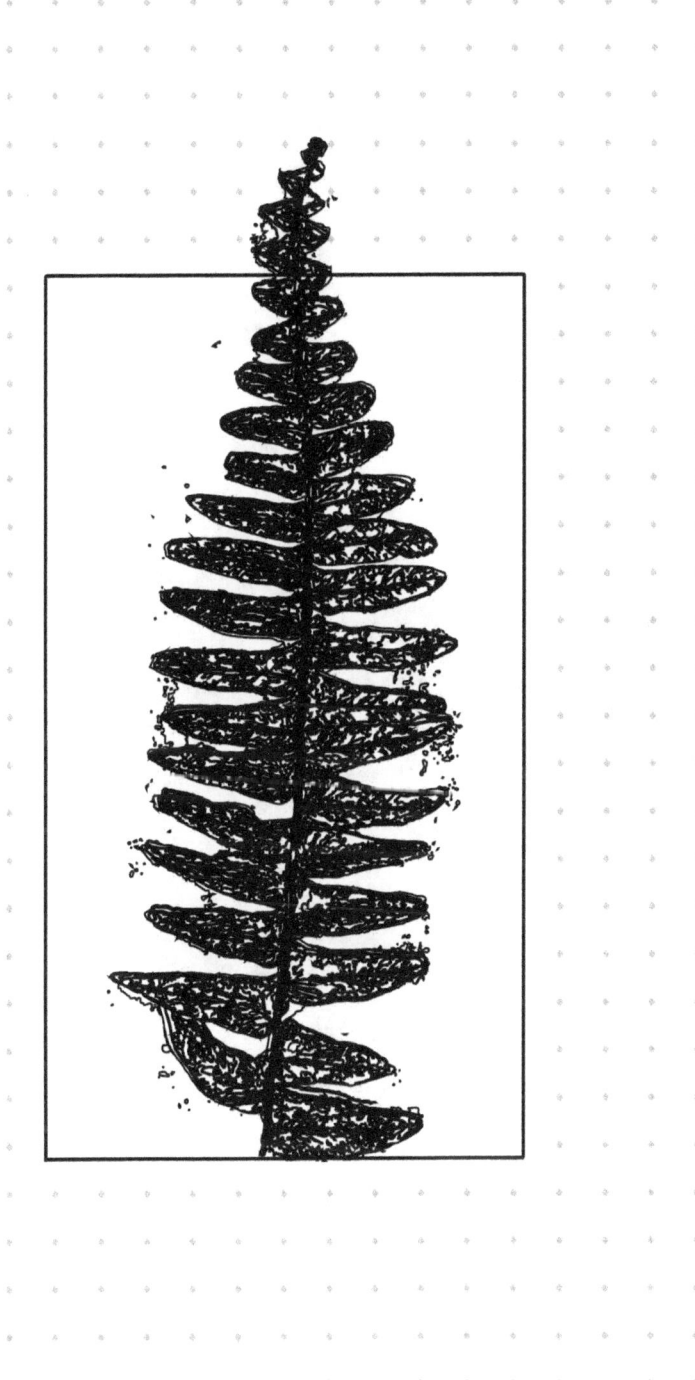

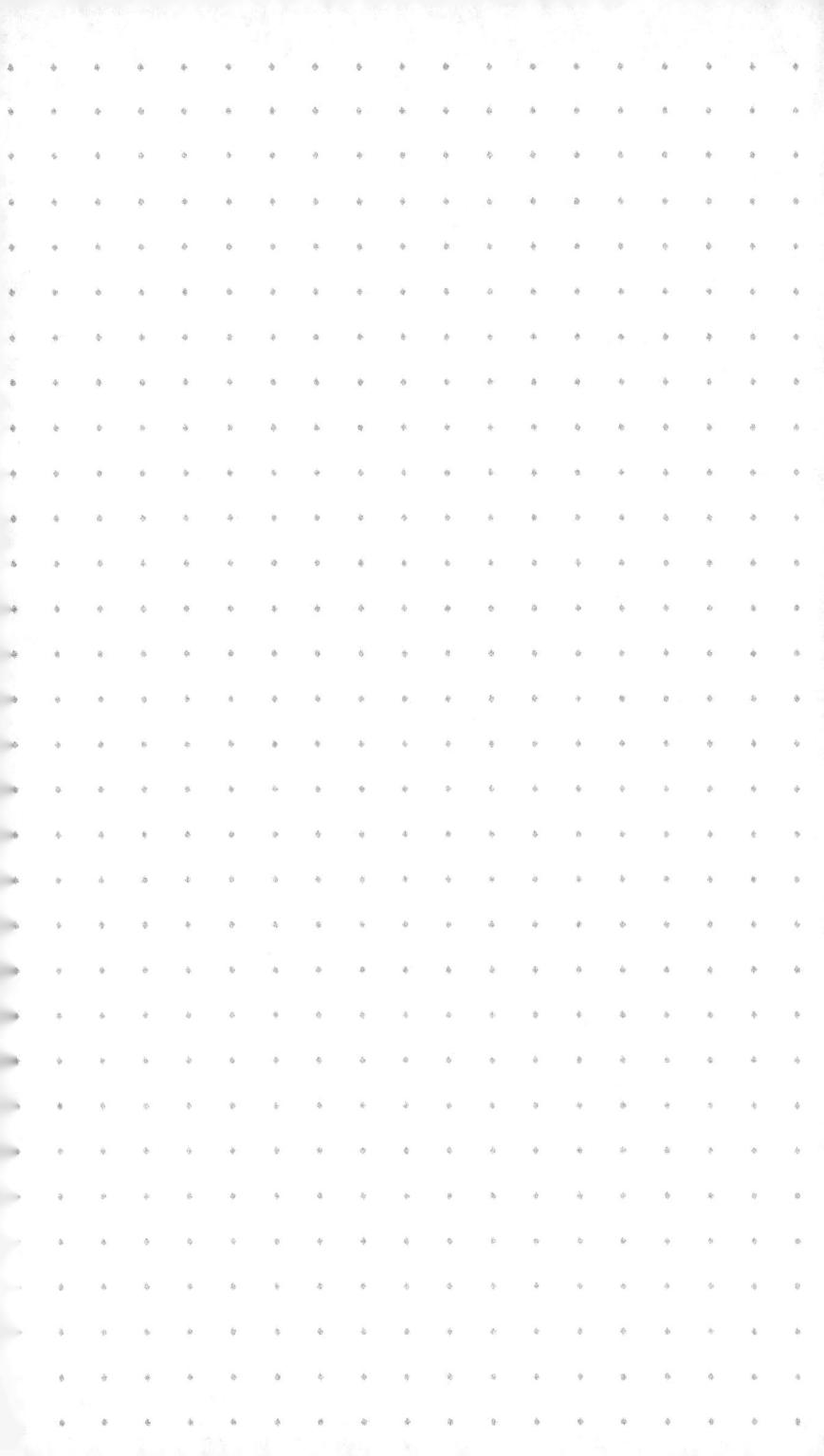

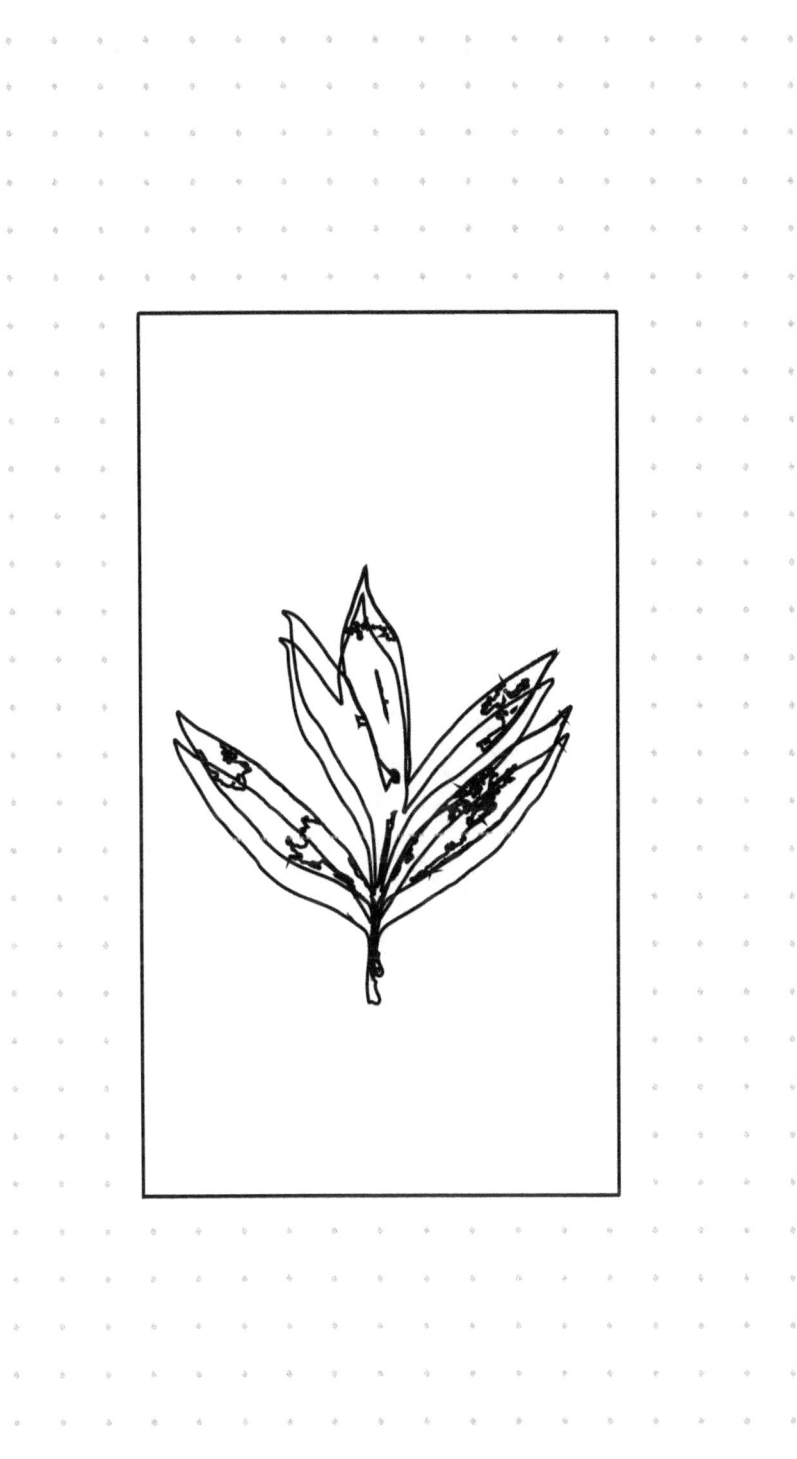

In me the caresser of life
I believe in those wing'd
purposes,

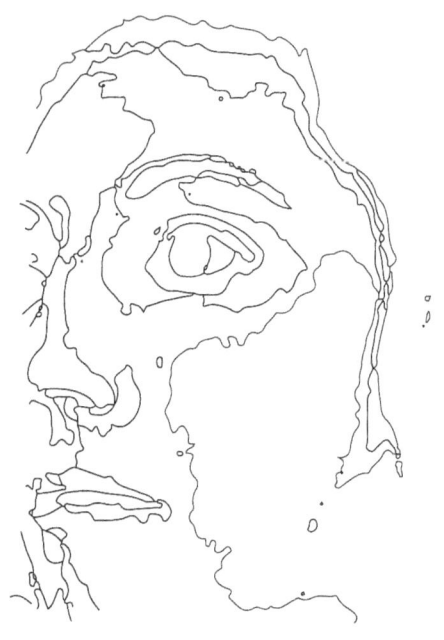

And again as I walk'd
the beach under
　　　the paling stars
　　of morning.

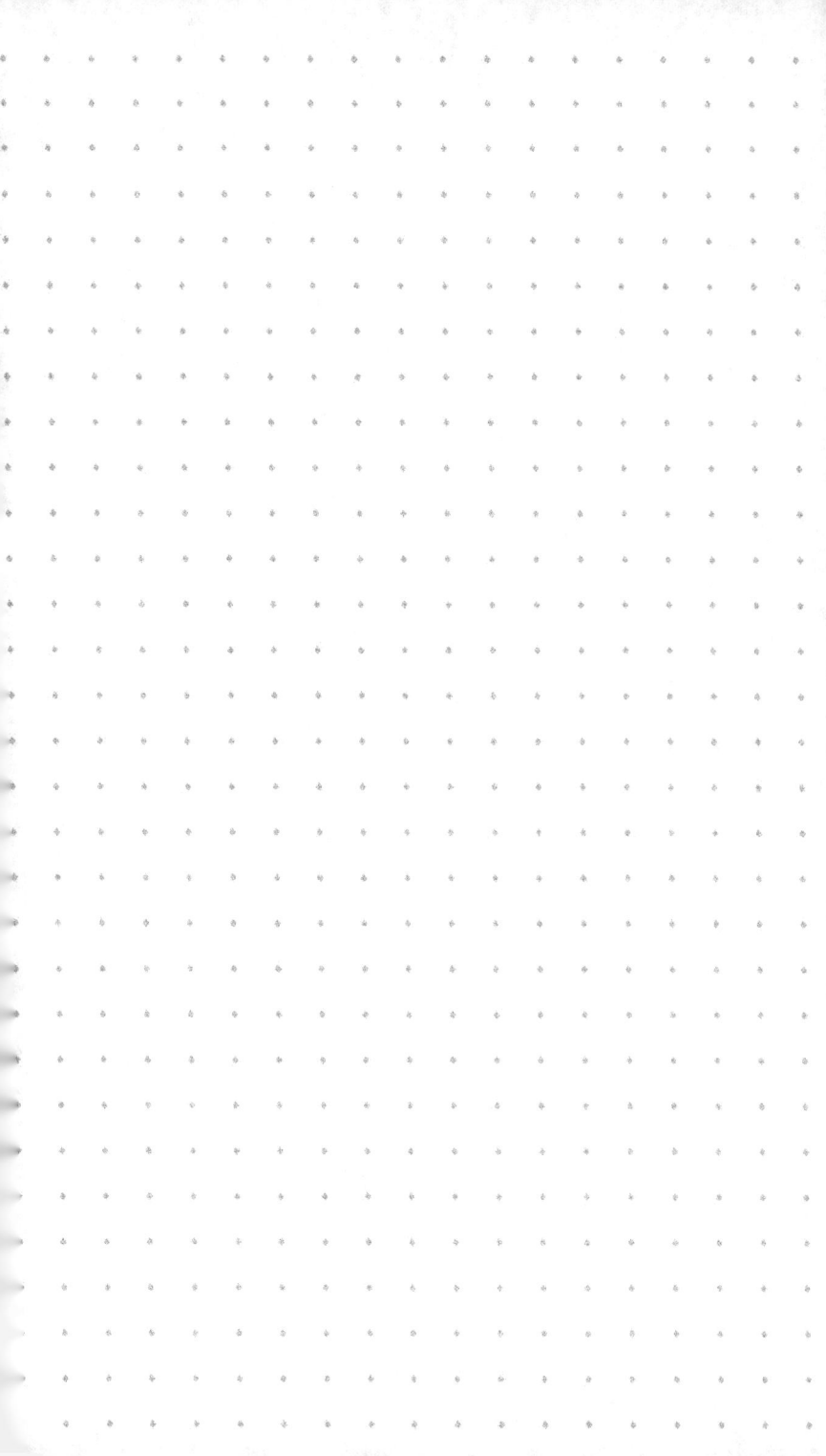

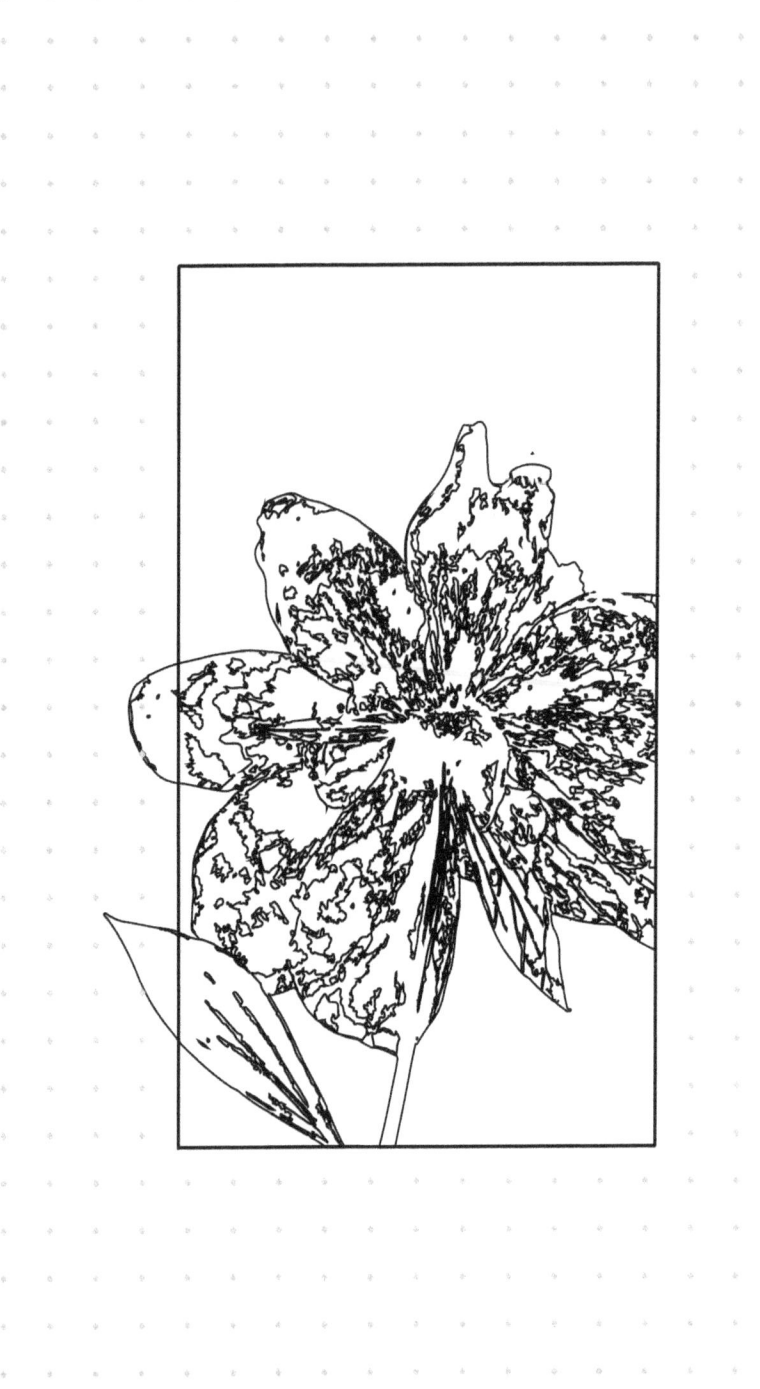

a dotted journal with freedom to dream

Dotted paper gives you the freedom to get your thoughts down on paper in whatever way makes sense. Write sideways, then upside down, or use thought bubbles and boxes to separate ideas.

...

Designed to promote healing, Michèle Saint-Michel's works encourage healthy coping and recovery from difficult experiences. The botanicals that appear were picked and pressed by the artist from the gardens around the log cabin where she works near the Missouri River in American's heartland.

This collection of journals is punctuated by the words of Walt Whitman. The poet's work was a pillar of Saint-Michel's erasure and concrete poetry collection, *Saint Agatha Mother Redeemer*. Working closely with the text created an intimacy in particular with his magnum opus, *Leaves of Grass*. Though it was first published in 1855, Whitman spent most of his professional life writing and rewriting the epic work. Take a page from Whitman and continue writing and rewriting your own story.

...

Also by Michèle Saint-Michel

Experiments in Dreaming: Lined Journal

A Journal of Gigantic Beauty: Lined Journal

Grief Is an Origami Swan

*Saint Agatha Mother Redeemer:
A Survivor's Story in the Words of Dead Poets*

Saint Agatha Mother Redeemer Coloring Book

Liner Notes for Getting Out Without Catching Fire

www.ingramcontent.com/pod-product-compliance
Lightning Source LLC
Chambersburg PA
CBHW070432010526
44118CB00014B/2014